Process Theology and Healing

Bruce Epperly

Energion Publications
Gonzalez, Florida
2023

ISBN: 978-1-63199-889-8
eISBN: 978-1-63199-890-4

Energion Publications
1241 Conference Rd
Cantonment, Florida 32533

pubs@energion.com
Energion.com

Table of Contents

Chapter One

A World Of Wonders

The power by which God sustains the world is the power of himself as the ideal...the world lives by its incarnation of God in itself.[1]

What does it mean to be healed? Can you be healed of illness without being cured? Where is God in the healing process? Do our prayers and spiritual practices make any difference in promoting healing? Can we join global and holistic spiritual practices with Western medicine? Can we claim miracles without supernaturalism? Questions like these can inspire hope and transform lives. They can also challenge our religious beliefs and images of God.

I've always been interested in the healing process, and the relationship between faith, sickness, and health. I grew up watching faith healers Oral Roberts and Kathryn Kuhlman on Sunday afternoons with my mother Loretta. In need of emotional healing, my mother took solace in Roberts' bombastic "Be healed" and Kuhlman's whispered "I believe in miracles." These pioneering televangelists believed that God would respond supernaturally to diseases of mind, body, spirit, and finances if we only had the faith of a mustard seed.

The son of a small-town Baptist pastor, I often companioned my father Everett Epperly on pastoral calls. I waited in the lobby while he visited congregants in the hospital, and I joined in prayers for healing at home visits. I overheard conversations about the power of prayer and also observed situations in which, despite desperate intercessions, a congregant died.

My mother had a kitchen magnet affixed to the refrigerator that promised, "prayer changes things." She believed that without divine intervention, she would have been the victim of the depression, low self-esteem, and obsessional thinking that plagued her throughout her life. My mother was a "prayer warrior," who

1 Alfred North Whitehead, *Religion in the Making* (New York: Macmillan, 1926),149.

depended on God to make a way through the wilderness of mental health issues.

As I child, I believed that God could intervene in our lives to heal body, mind, and spirit. Yet, I wondered why some were healed and others continued to deal with chronic illness or succumbed to death, despite our prayers.

Although I no longer believe that God acts supernaturally, from outside the world to overturn the laws of nature, I am deeply interested in the healing process, whether it involves answers to prayer, divine activity, antibiotics and vaccines, surgery, chemotherapy, energy work, or the importance of self-care. At some point in our lives, we all need healing, and the impact of a power, energy, and wisdom greater than our own to restore us to wholeness. Now an adult theologian, I recognize that "healing" refers to the whole person, while "curing" relates to a particular disease or malady. I now see healing as a relational as well as personal issue. I want to be on the side of healing, the wholeness of persons and institutions, and believe that God is present in our prayers as well in the lives of healthcare professionals developing pharmaceuticals that saved millions of lives during the COVID epidemic and whose dedication led to curing once incurable diseases such as certain forms of cancers, polio, and HIV. I meditate, and also medicate for hypertension, and get flu, shingles, pneumonia, and COVID vaccines, grateful for God's Creativity inspiring human creativity.

As a pastor and friend, I have sought to be a healing companion, incarnating in my relationships and ministry God's aim at wholeness and Shalom. I have been a companion in the healing of friends, family, and congregants. I have sat at the bedsides of dying congregants and friends, who no longer prayed for a cure, but sought peace of mind and the cessation of pain at the end of life's journey.

The healing I seek for myself and others no longer involves the supernatural interventions of a distant God, requiring prayer and adoration to act. Prayer is not magic, nor does it force God's hand. God is not omnipotent, nor are our prayers, in healing the sick. As a child, I lived in a God-filled world in which healing was built into the fabric of the universe. I felt that Jesus walked beside me, and I knew Jesus was involved in the interplay of medical care and prayerful concern, both of which were inspired by God's creative love. Poet Walt Whitman once declared that "all is miracle," and I believe that there is enough miracle to go around in the divinely guided and open-ended processes of nature to enable us to shape our health and well-being in amazing and unexpected ways. We are filled with awe at the miracles of medicine, curing illnesses that would have been fatal less than twenty years ago, and we experience a similar amazement when we see persons transformed physically and spiritually through prayer, meditative practices, energy work, and shamanic rituals. The natural world of cause and effect is miraculous, and the curative powers of our bodies astound us. We see only the tip of the iceberg in terms of God's presence in the world and in the power of the mind, spirit, and creativity, to heal our cells and souls.

There is More. Before the voyages of Columbus, the edges of maps bore the inscription, *ne plus ultra,* "there is no more." After the ambiguous and, in many ways, tragic "discovery" of the new world, cartographers revised their maps with the words, *plus ultra,* "there is more," despite the fact that European voyagers had no idea of the wonders of the new continent and, in their lack of moral imagination, treated the land and its inhabitants as material to be exploited rather than gifts of their Creator to be reverenced and respected. Today, the words *plus ultra,* "there is more," apply to the realm of healing and medicine. Just as the horizons of healing expanded beyond folk remedies and bloodletting in the twentieth century with the advent of chemical therapies, robotic surgery, C-T scans, and transfusions, today the vistas of healing have expanded to be global in nature, embracing both "high tech" and "high touch," the marvels of technology and miracles of human touch and mystical experience. The same hospital systems that employ MRI imaging and immunotherapy now sponsor therapeutic and Reiki healing touch practitioners and classes in meditation for palliation and stress reduction and participate in studies involving the use of hallucinogens to provide spiritual care and calm for persons facing life-threatening illness. Death doulas, midwives of transition, convey spiritual resources that enable persons at the edges of life to see death as adventure and not a tragedy.

We don't have to choose between spirituality and medicine. New visions of the universe and human life reveal the intimacy of mind, body, and spirit, and call us to a truly holistic vision of health and disease, and prevention and response.

These are, as singer-songwriter Paul Simon, intones, "the days of miracle and wonder," both small and large. Many of us have experienced healing as a result of prayer, the use of affirmations, energy work, and the laying on of hands in worship services. We may have experienced the presence of a Power and Love greater than our own providing comfort, guidance, and healing, when we reached the limits of our abilities. We are also living longer and healthier lives and many are, frankly, alive because of amazing leaps in Western technological medicine, especially in the areas of cancer, HIV, and other diseases which are now curable or chronic, whereas once they spelled death. Sometimes the healings we experience are undramatic, other times they turn our world upside down dramatically.

Process theology recognizes the ambiguity of all medical advances, and equally affirms that in going beyond binary and dualistic approaches to health care, we can employ a variety of medical approaches, ancient and modern, surgical and non-invasive, somatic and spiritual, to promote overall longevity and well-being. Process theology also recognizes that health and illness are also related to economics, environment, and accessibility, and that in the interdependence of life, the health of each of us depends on the health of all of us and that we must seek to promote a healthy environment and strive toward the equalizing of health care availability and economic justice.

Healing Moments. Grounded in the vision of an interdependent universe, human agency, and an ever-present God, process theology asserts that God is always on the side of healing and wholeness. The Great Physician aims at beauty and health in body, mind, spirit, relationships, and environment. Although the healing process may, at times, be painful physically, emotionally, and spiritually, God is on our side. God is out to heal, and not to hurt, to comfort and not condemn. Wherever there is truth and healing, God is its ultimate source.

The growing importance of spirit-based and energy-related healing is demonstrated by the formation in 1991 of National Center for Complementary and Integrative Health, a branch of the National Institutes of Health. Science is studying the sacred, and has found that prayer, meditation, and energy medicine contribute to persons' well-being and can be used to supplement and complement Western technological medicine.

Still, some moments are "thin places" of healing power, where God's presence and human openness meet in healings that transform persons' lives. We don't understand the mechanics of such healing events, despite their impact of our lives. In the next few paragraphs, I will be relating accounts of the impact of spiritual healing on persons' lives, recognizing that mind, body, and spirit, are interdependent and constantly shape one another. These are anecdotal but nevertheless transformative of the persons involved. To those who have experienced the Great Physician's healing touch, these events were "miraculous" in a world in which naturalistic "miracles" are built into the fabric of reality.

United Methodist minister and spiritual guide Tilda Norberg tells of an experiment in healing she performed on a patient who communicated only in "word salad" — meaningless words strung together. For a while Norberg had felt God's lure to "put my hands on someone and pray for healing." The man seemed like the perfect subject, since if she failed, no one would notice. Norberg describes her experience, "As soon as I put my hands on his head, he stopped talking. I prayed a very simple prayer, 'O God, please heal whatever caused this man to withdraw like this. In Jesus' name. Amen." As soon as I took my hands away, he started jabbering again, and I breathed a sigh of relief. Good, it hadn't worked and I was off the hook." Several weeks later, she was confronted by a hospital therapist who asked, "What did you do to that man?" Stunned, Norberg confessed that she had prayed for him. She was amazed when the therapist told her that the man began to speak normally later that day and reported that "the chaplain prayed for me." He was later discharged from the hospital. Norberg was convinced that God truly answered prayers, began to actively pray for persons in need, and became a leader in healing ministries within mainstream and progressive Christianity.[2]

One Friday afternoon, my mother-in-law Maxine experienced an excruciating toothache. Realizing that the dental offices were closed, and that she would have to wait at least three days for treatment, she asked me to give her a reiki healing touch treatment. I laid hands on her jaw, opening to the Energy of Love flowing through us. Within minutes, her pain disappeared, and she was pain-free for five days until she could receive a dental appointment. She still needed dental work, but she claimed in her words that "it was the reiki that made all the difference in the world. When Bruce touched me, the pain stopped, and I could go about my business without any discomfort."

Diane came to me, as her university pastor, debilitated by migraine headaches that came without warning and made day-to-day living a struggle. I prayed with Diane, taught her a form of centering prayer which involved the repetition of a meaningful word along with breath prayer, slow prayerful breathing to open her to God's Spirit. I also gave her a reiki treatment and then gave her several distant reiki treatments during scheduled times of meditation. I didn't promise supernatural intervention, but assured Diane that she would now have a spiritual tool to reduce her pain and help her be an agent, rather than a victim, in responding to the migraines. After practicing the techniques that I taught her, Diane began to have fewer and less severe headaches, and now is migraine-free. She calls her healing a "miracle," something she could not have imagined prior to her sessions with me.

Looking back at my childhood, I recall my father Everett testifying to the healing of a hernia, during the 1950's, a time in which recovery from hernia surgery often took weeks. In the midst of the challenges of ministry and family life, he felt he couldn't afford to be "on the shelf." As the hymn counsels, he "took it to the Lord in prayer." His discomfort ceased immediately, and when he returned to the doctor, his physician found him physically sound.

---

2 Tilda Norberg and Robert Webber, *Stretch Out Your Hand: Exploring Healing Prayer* (Nashville: Upper Room Books, 1998), 13-14.

These stories reveal the relationship between spirituality and healing. Over the years, I have heard hundreds of testimonies involving the impact of laying on of hands, Reiki healing touch, and intercessory prayer in unexpected and, in the eyes of those healed, "miraculous" cures of cancer, heart disease, debilitating anxiety, and learning disabilities. Unexplainable solely by medical science, the recipients of these healings affirm they were personally transformed and point to the presence of Spirit, faith, energy, and hope in the healing process. They reveal the activity of a force toward wholeness within our cells and souls that complements technological medicine and promotes our personal agency in responding to illness as well as maintaining good health. There is an arc that bends toward healing congruent with the arc aiming toward justice. Such healings are not unilateral, nor solely the result of one factor such as medication or prayer. They reflect the presence of a movement toward health and wholeness operating within the cause-and-effect relationships of our lives. Such healings also reflect the impact of the faith factor, and the belief in a divine healing congruent with the medical recognition that meditation, the placebo effect, and religious participation and volunteer activities promote health and well-being and recovery from illness.

Your Theology Has Made You Whole. Process theology is healing theology. Process theology provides the vision of a living universe, where all life is interconnected, and spirit is embodied and the body is inspired. Our minds shape our bodies, our bodies shape our minds. While not omnipotent, our faith can make us whole. What we believe radiates throughout our bodies, healing our cells as well as our soul. God is on our side, aiming at wholeness, growth, and beauty. In the world described by process theology, undramatic and dramatic healing experiences can occur as expressions of the deeper laws of nature, in the intersection of God's call, human response, spiritual practices, and medical care. Nature is miraculous enough that we don't need to invoke supernatural and arbitrary interventions of a distant, otherwise apathetic God. God is here with us in our cells and spirits and when we open to God's vision, God's energy of life, healing energy bursts forth.

Process theology says "yes" to God's vision of healing and our partnership in healing our bodies, minds, spirits, and the planet. Yet, with every "yes" comes a "no," a challenge to theologies that harm rather than heal, blame rather than empower, and promote passivity rather than agency in the interplay of sickness and health. Tragically, irresponsible and heartless theology can kill bodies as well as spirits. This is true not only in the anti-science movements within Christianity, but also in: 1) theological beliefs that blame the victim for their illness, 2) see illness as a divine visitation or test of our faith, 3) believe sickness is a punishment for sin, 4) reflects God's all-powerful will, and 5) in stark contrast to the belief in divine omnipotence, is entirely the result of our choices and behaviors. Briefly put, such theologies either view health and illness as completely a matter of divine decision in terms of either omnipotence, testing, and predestination; rewards and punishment based on our behavior; or created entirely by our own agency, whether we focus on the faith of the individual as all-determining as suggested in certain Christian circles or assert "you create your own reality," a belief held in many new age and new spirituality circles. In the latter case, when we become sick or do not experience healing, we are blamed for lacking faith or harboring negativity.

Process theology, as we will see in future chapters, avoids the extremes of impotence and omnipotence, either in terms of our or of God's agency. Process theology affirms a multi-factorial vision of healing in which health and wholeness is the result of the interplay of many factors: lifestyle, choices, environment, DNA, genetic inheritance, environment and economics, family of origin, communities, and God's ever-present aim at wholeness. Most importantly, process theology affirms that God is out to heal us, not harm us, and that God's aim for us is abundant life in the context of creating just and healthy societies and congregations.

Process Healing

Theology and spirituality are profoundly connected. Our theologies and religious traditions emerged from transcendent, paranormal, and mystical experiences, in which persons experienced the Holy as a lived reality. In the evolution of religious experience, encountering the Holy often led to physical healing as well as spiritual transformation and political liberation. Historically, mystics — Hebraic prophets/judges, shaman, medicine persons — were also healers and mediated the healing Energy of Love to their communities.

Inherently spiritual in nature, process theology helps us understand the relationship of Divinity and healing, and challenges toxic understandings of health and disease. Accordingly, each chapter concludes with healing practices, grounded in the insights of process theology.

In this first practice, our goal is to make the healing process concrete and relevant to your life. Recognizing that God is constantly inspiring us, begin with a time of stillness, breathing deeply God's peace that passes all understanding. Let the peace of God fill your body, mind, and spirit. When you begin to experience God's presence deep in your spirit, reflect on where you need God's healing touch. What aspects of your life are diseased, broken, or blocked, and in need of divine transformation? "Ask, seek, and knock" for God's Energy of Love to heal your life (Matthew 7:7-8). You may receive insight in regards to spiritual practices and practitioners that will promote your healing — spiritual guides, energy workers and Reiki practitioners, massage therapists, psychotherapists, herbalists, other complementary healers, or medical specialists, or a combination of these.

In a second practice, after a time of quiet reflection, ask for God's wisdom in terms of someone who needs your prayers. When you receive guidance, take time to pray for this person, once or many times, using a prayer of your choice, or these words, "God, may your healing touch rest upon _____, bringing them joy and abundant life. Fill them with the peace that comes from knowing your blessing. Amen." Your prayer could be a tipping point, concentrating divine energy in ways that bring wholeness to one for whom you pray.

Chapter Two

Process Theology as Holistic Theology

> *In fact, the world beyond is so intimately entwined in our own natures that unconsciously we identify our more vivid experiences of it with ourselves... but the body is part of the external world, continuous with it. In which it is just as much a part of nature as anything else there — a river, or a mountain, or a cloud. Also, if we are fussily exact, we cannot define where a body begins and where external nature ends... the human body is that region of the world which is the primary field of human expressions.*[3]

The naturalistic vision of health and healing described by process theology takes us beyond dualism, individualism, and divine supernatural intervention, and awakens us to the significance of spiritual practices and attitude in health and wellbeing. In contrast to modern medicine, grounded in the mind-body dualism articulated by Rene Descartes and the mechanistic worldview championed by Newtonian physics, and descriptive of health and illness primarily in terms of isolated, individual human bodies, process theology maintains that the relationship of mind, spirit, and community are essential factors in health and illness. Humans are part of a lively, dynamic, integrated, and spirit-filled universe in which healing practices, religious and personal attitudes, and relationships can be a matter of life and death. In contrast to the distant, arbitrary God, described by supernaturalism and deism, process theology sees God as intimate, ever-present, and loving, and seeking our well-being in every situation. Dramatic healing occurs through the confluence of divine and human intentionality and healing communities, often in the context of medical diagnosis and care.

3 Alfred North Whitehead, *Modes of Thought* (New York: Free Press, 1968), 22-23.

Process theology presents a series of affirmations about the nature of reality and human life which can transform your cells as well as your spirit. In this section, I outline several key ideas of the process-relational vision of the universe and human existence. I state these ideas in terms of affirmations of the spirit, positive statements that describe our world and promote well-being for persons whose lives are guided by these affirmations.

» *The World is Alive.* We live in a vital and dynamic universe. Energy and experience course through all things, including our bodies. Psalm 148 proclaims the process-relational vision of a living universe in which all occasions of experience praise their Companion and Creator.

Praise him, sun and moon;
  praise him, all you shining stars!
Praise him, you highest heavens
  and you waters above the heavens Let them praise the name of the Lord…
Praise the Lord from the earth,
  you sea monsters and all deeps,
fire and hail, snow and frost,
  stormy wind fulfilling his command!...
Wild animals and all cattle,
  creeping things and flying birds!
Kings of the earth and all peoples,
  princes and all rulers of the earth!
Young men and women alike,
  old and young together! (Psalm 148:4-11, sections)

Our bodies are miraculous in their creativity and intensity of experience. Our cells shout praises as they provide protection, and facilitate respiration, circulation, and sight. A living universe and living bodies are sensitive and responsive to their environment in contrast to the unfeeling and mechanical physical and embodied world described by Newton and Descartes. In a living universe, the heavens declare the glory of God and so do our respiratory and immune systems. God's presence is experienced everywhere. "Let everything that breathes praise God" as God breathes through everything. (Psalm 150:6) In a pan-experiential universe, sacrament and spirituality are not restricted to religious institutions and their clergy or the human mind, they resonate through all creation, enlivening and energizing the non-human as well as the embodied human world. A living universe inspires respect and reverence, whether we are relating to another person's body or to coral reefs and Right Whales.

» *The World is Saved by Beauty.* The aim of the universe, according to Alfred North Whitehead, is toward the production of beauty, described in terms of the interplay of order and novelty, and creativity and intensity of experience. Anyone who sees photographs from the Webb and Hubble telescopes or microscopic views of the cells of our bodies or the eye of grasshopper is astonished at the wonders of creation. The Psalmist proclaims that we are awesomely and wonderfully made, and that affirmation applies to all creation. (Psalm 139:14) The calling of human life and the many varieties of medicine, East and West, is toward the promotion of beauty, aiming to do "something beautiful for God," as Mother (Saint) Teresa counsels. Behold, the body is holy, the body-mind-spirit continuum is beautiful, our senses and the world we see are wonderful, and worthy of celebration in all its diversity.

» *We are Connected.* Process-relational theology takes us beyond dualism and individualism. Mind and body are intertwined and cannot be separated. What happens in our emotional, mental, intellectual, and spiritual lives shapes our physical health, and our physical health shapes our mental, intellectual, emotional, and spiritual well-being. Moreover, we cannot speak of individuals, whether persons, trees, coral reefs, or cells, apart from their environment. Health and illness have a communal and environmental component. Physician Kenneth Pelletier aptly titled one of his books, *Healthy People in Unhealthy Places: Stress and Fitness at Work.* Our workplaces and working conditions can promote health or sickness and can be toxic or salubrious. Economic and educational opportunities have been found to be factors in a person's long-term health condition. Stress-related illnesses are more pervasive in inner-city impoverished neighborhoods than suburbs, regardless of race. Hippocrates associated seasons, prevailing winds, and the quality of the air and water with the occurrence of disease. Twenty-four centuries after Hippocrates, we are keenly aware of the impact of the environment — as well as diet — on physical and emotional well-being. In an interdependent universe, all health is public health, and we must consider climate change and environmental quality as well as diet and exercise as factors in health and disease. Loving and faithful environments are factors in unexpected as well as gradual healings. In a relational world, intercessory prayer as a form of non-local or distant intentionality shapes the experiences of persons across the globe as well as right next to us.

» *The Body is Inspired and the Mind is Embodied.* Contrary to Rene Descartes' mind-body dualism, the body is vibrant and alive, and the mind emerges in relationship to body that supports it. Every moment of experience, according to Whitehead, has both a mental and physical pole, that is, an element of possibility and creativity as well as physical inheritance. There is a continuum of experience that connects our most creative thinking with the amazing surveillance and protective abilities of T-cells in our immune system. Meditation as well as medication is a factor in reducing hypertension. Chemical imbalances shape our emotional lives, and emotional stress impacts our physical well-being. Positive attitudes energize our immune system, while hopelessness depresses immunity. The body, like the universe, is alive, sentient, and continuous with the mind. We feel joy and delight in our cells as well as our souls. Eric Liddell rejoices that "God made me fast, and when I run, I can feel God's pleasure." Spiritual practices and religious rituals, such as contemplative prayer, visualization, affirmations, and healing touch can, in remarkable ways, transform our physical and spiritual lives. Meditative prayer produces the "relaxation response," reducing stress and physical pain and promoting overall wellbeing. The body also remembers childhood emotional trauma. Traumatic anxiety can be elicited by stressful encounters, reminding us in our cells as well as spirit of past experiences of vulnerability and abuse. Accordingly, we can promote physical well-being through the spiritual "healing of memories," psychotherapy, and communal prayer. We can visualize Jesus beside us, protecting us, during times of trauma. Prayerful and safe companions, including companion animals, can elicit the wellsprings of healing, and enable persons to function with confidence and calm. We can change our physical health by changing our attitudes and engaging in spiritual practices. As physician Dale Matthews asserts, prayer and Prozac joined together can transform a person's life. I would add meditation and medication, chanting and chemotherapy, and faith and pharmaceuticals.

» *We are Agents of Our Destiny.* In contrast to Western medicine which has often emphasized passivity in relationship to illness and medical care, process-relational theology affirms agency in every aspect of life. We are not victims of the world we experience, nor are we victims of our past limitations and trauma. Change is possible: faith, openness to God, and loving support can inspire agency that liberates us from the negative impact of past experiences. Even our cells respond creatively to their environment. With the ability to respond comes the ability to bring forth possibilities out of the concrete limitations we face. We have, as Viktor Frankl asserts, the freedom in any situation and the ability "to choose one's attitude in any given set of circumstances, to choose one's own way." Further, Frankl affirms, "when we are no longer able to change a situation, we are challenged to change ourselves." We are not victims, but healers; we are not passive recipients, but active agents in our healing and wholeness. We can bring spiritual, emotional, and relational healing to our lives through commitment to meditative practices, energy work, dietary changes, the use of affirmations, participation in healing services, changed behaviors, and the use of certain hallucinogens which have been associated with stress reduction and self-transcendence enabling persons to face their mortality with hope and confidence. While there may not always be a physical cure, there is always potential for healing through spiritual practices and the love of friends and family.

» *God is On Your Side.* Process theology asserts that God is always seeking the best possibilities for us and the world. Many theological perspectives assert that God is responsible, either directly or indirectly, for disease, debilitation, destruction, and death. Popular author Rick Warren asserts that every event in our lives from our family of origin, physical and emotional challenges, DNA, and apparently accidental events is "father filtered" and comes from God's hand to test our commitment to our Creator. The Calvinist tradition states that God has planned in advance everything that occurs in our lives: cancer, heart disease, ALS, car accidents, are all rooted in God's eternal and unchanging providence. We have no control about matters of health, life, or death. Other theologians believe that God "allows" life-shattering suffering to occur to provide room for personal decision-making. Yet, the suffering that God allows is often greater than our resources and appears to have no redemptive value.[4] In contrast, process theology describes God's power in the world as grounded in love. Indeed, God's very nature is to be loving toward creation as a whole as well as to individuals. God's goal is beauty and intensity of experience, appropriate to each moment of our lives and the context in which we live. A Truly Loving Parent is not coercive or omnipotent but seeks abundant life for us and all creation. When the apostle Paul proclaims that "in all things God works for good," he declares that God's aim at goodness pertains to every aspect of our lives, physical, emotional, intellectual, relational, and spiritual (Romans 8:28). God works within the tragedy and suffering of life — tragedies God does not cause and suffering God experiences -- to bring forth beauty, health, and personal growth. God's quest for Shalom embraces the personal and the political, aiming at healing persons, institutions, economics, the soul of the

4 One of the most insightful treatments of God's role in suffering is Thomas Jay Oord's *God Can't: How to Believe in God and Love after Tragedy, Abuse, and Other Evils* (Boise, Idaho: SacraSage Press, 2019). I reflect on the problem the relationship of God and suffering in *Finding God in Suffering: A Journey with Job* (Gonzalez, FL: Energion Publications, 2014).

nation, and the health of the planet. The Great Physician provides multiple personal, medical, spiritual, and political pathways to heal ourselves and the earth and invites us to be God's companions in the healing process.

- *You Matter to God.* Alfred North Whitehead, the philosophical parent of process theology, describes God as "the fellow sufferer who understands." God is also the intimate companion who celebrates. Whereas many theological perspectives view God as the "unmoved mover," dwelling in unchanging perfection, immune from the sufferings of the world and apathetic in terms of our personal suffering, process theology affirms the divine pathos. God is the ultimate empath, the most moved mover. God not only touches all creation with love. Moreover, creation touches the divine heart. Our pain is God's pain. Our despair is God's despair. Our grief is God's lamentation. Our joy is God's joy. God is not overwhelmed by the pain of the world. Rather, God responds to the world with the Energy of Love and the Vision of Possibility that gives birth to our own creativity, compassion, and challenge as well as the ongoing emergence and evolution of healing practices. The process affirmation, "God in all things, all things in God," portrays God's intimate creative-responsive love. The one who gives birth to the universe and guides the process of evolution is also the one who seeks our healing and wholeness. The one whose love embraces all creation feels our joys and sorrows as if they God's own and provides pathways to wholeness and remedies to disease.

Process Healing

Theological reflection involves focusing on spiritual affirmations, grounded in our understanding of the relationship of God and the world, our identity as God's beloved children, and God's loving, creative, and empowering presence, power, and providence in our lives. My daily spiritual practices include contemplative prayer, breath prayers, Reiki healing touch, and intercessory prayer. Along with these spiritual practices, I recite spiritual affirmations throughout the day to guide my path and awaken me to my role as an agency furthering the moral and spiritual arcs of the universe in my personal and community life. When practiced regularly, spiritual affirmations heal negative self-talk that contributes to emotional, intellectual, and physical disease. In healing the mind through affirmations, we begin to heal our bodies. Affirmations begin with the intellect and conscious mind and then over time radiate to transform our unconscious responses, memories, behavioral responses, and physical well-being. My spiritual practice includes scripture-based affirmations, congruent with process theology:

> Nothing can separate me from the love of God.
>
> God will supply all my needs.
>
> I let go of limitations and open to divine possibilities.
>
> I bless everyone I see.
>
> God's light flows through me.
>
> I am the light of the world.
>
> I am an instrument of God's peace.
>
> God's healing power flows in and through me.

You can begin to utilize your own spiritual affirmations by considering where you need to grow and find healing, and then create positive statements to respond to your deepest personal needs, knowing that our quest for God awakens us to new energies and wisdom.

Chapter Three

Jesus The Healer: A Process Perspective

When the Western world accepted Christianity, Caesar conquered... The brief Galilean vision of humility flickered through the ages, uncertainly... the Galilean vision...does not emphasize the ruling Caesar or the ruthless moralist, or the unmoved mover. It dwells upon the tender elements of the world which slowly and in quietness operate by love; and it finds its purpose in the present immediacy of a kingdom not of this world. Love neither rules, nor is it unmoved; also it is a little oblivious to morals. It does not look to the future; but finds its own reward in the immediate present.[5]

With the rise of global and complementary medicine, the role of Jesus the healer has become a focus within and beyond Christianity. No longer is Christian healing ministry the province of "holy rollers" and Pentecostals. Mainstream and progressive congregations sponsor healing services and seek to integrate Jesus' healing ministry with Reiki healing touch, therapeutic touch, yoga, and other energy-based healing modalities as well as the therapies of Western medicine. The role of faith in well-being has been explored in terms of the "faith factor" and the "placebo effect." Further, the significance of compassion and hospitality as complementary to science in the healing process leads me, and other medical commentators, to view Jesus and Hippocrates as the joint founders of Western medicine.

During his ministry, Jesus was known as a healer and spirit person, who could transform persons' cells and souls, and empower his followers to become healers themselves. Jesus' twin mission

5 Alfred North Whitehead, *Process and Reality: Corrected Edition* (New York: Free Press, 1978), 342-343.

statements point to the centrality of healing in Jesus' ministry. Quoting the prophet Isaiah, Jesus asserts:

> The Spirit of the Lord is upon me, because he has anointed me to bring good news to the poor. He has sent me to proclaim release to the captives and recovery of sight to the blind, to let the oppressed go free, to proclaim the year of the Lord's favor. (Luke 4:18-19)

Jesus also proclaimed that he "came that they may have life and have it abundantly" (John 10:10). Jesus confronted anything that stood in the way of human well-being, whether its origin was political, religious, physical, or reflected the activity of malevolent spiritual forces. Jesus' love liberated the healing energies residing in those who have been marginalized and excluded as a result of disease, ethnicity, and occupation.

Mystic encounters with the Living God, or the Holy Energy of Life, are at the heart of healing practices. Jesus' healing power emerged from his intimacy with God. Without delving too deeply into the intricacies of process Christology, we can affirm that while the world lives by the incarnation of God, giving birth to each moment of experience, some moments and persons more fully reflect God's vision than others. God can choose to be more active in certain persons and situations, based on our openness, the social and religious context, and the interplay of divine call and human response. Process theology can affirm that God "chose" Jesus to fully reveal God's vision of Shalom and Wholeness and also that Jesus responded to God's call, aligning himself fully with God's healing and prophetic vision, and releasing by his openness to God, the healing energy of the universe. The stories of the angelic visitation to Mary and the bestowal of the Spirit at Jesus' baptism point to the early Christian movement's recognition that Jesus was uniquely anointed by God to be the messenger of healing, reconciliation, and spiritual transformation. While unique in nature, the Incarnation in Jesus of Nazareth is natural, rather than supernatural. According to process theology, the "natural" world is far more dynamic and energetic than we can imagine. Jesus' life is not the violation of the laws of nature, but their fullest expression. Fully alive, Jesus revealed God's glory and provides a pathway for us to experience the fullness of God's presence in our lives. The world lives by the incarnation of

God and the healing power mediated by Jesus is available to everyone who awakens to God's Energy of Love flowing in their lives and all creation. As the reflection of God's universal aim at healing, wholeness, and beauty, Jesus' mission complements God's unique presence in every world-transforming spiritual leader and spiritual movement. Indeed, with full fidelity to Jesus as Healer and Savior, we can affirm that wherever truth and healing are present God is its source, whether in Qigong or Reiki or chemotherapy and surgery.[6]

Scripture proclaims that God loves the world, and this includes our bodies as well as our minds and spirits. The Incarnation affirms that healing embraces the whole person and their relationships. Jesus healed persons by eliciting and intensifying the divine healing resources resident in all creation using a variety of healing modalities, congruent with today's holistic healing practices as well as Shamans and healers throughout the ages: healing touch, intensification of energy, faith or the placebo effect, loving words, affirming the humanity of outcasts, challenging social and religious ostracism, joining medicine and spirituality (spittle), creating healing communities, prayer, and confronting demonic powers (exorcism).

Jesus' healing ministry expressed his divine empathy. Like his Divine Parent, Jesus was "the fellow sufferer who understands" and the intimate companion who celebrates.

Among Jesus' healings, four stories stand out as representative of Jesus' naturalistic transformation of cells, souls, and communities. When a woman with a flow of blood, that rendered her "unclean" and marginalized socially and religiously in her community touches Jesus as object of faith, a power flows from Jesus that cures her ailment. Jesus is a transformer of energy (prana, chi, dunamis) elevating the Energy of Love to bring new life to bodies as well as spirits (Mark 5:35-43). When Jesus heals Jairus' daughter, he banishes the naysayers, creating an affirmative community, as the prelude to awakening her with healing words. To a man born blind, Jesus administers a common first-century remedy, spittle, along with prayers for healing, intensifying the power of nature to restore his sight (John 9:1-7. At the pool of Siloam, Jesus asks a man who had experienced paralysis for decades, "Do you want to be healed?"

6 For more on Christology, see Bruce Epperly, *Messy Incarnation: Meditations on Christ in Process* (Gonzalez, FL: Energion, 2022).

The man stands up, first, on the inside, and then by his own agency, his body, mind, and spirit are transformed through trusting God rather than his own incapacity. Later in the day, after Jesus views the man denying his own role in the healing process, Jesus warns him that his continued healing is grounded in maintaining a positive attitude and sense of responsibility, rather than succumbing to passive acceptance of fate. Jesus believed that although faith is not all-determining, agency and responsibility reflect our responses to God's graceful and loving healing power (John 5:2-18).

As a spiritual person, Jesus believed that God had a bias toward healing. In Whitehead's words, the teleology of the universe is aimed at beauty. There is a global arc toward wholeness, or Shalom, in our bodies and spirits. Accordingly, as Jesus declares in responding to the request to heal a man who had been sight-impaired from birth that God does not cause illness. Disease and diminishment are the results of many factors, including DNA, inheritance, environment, social limitations, decision-making. Working in our lives, in the intricacies of our cells, organs, emotions, and thought processes, God seeks our well-being, the "best for that impasse." While God works lovingly and non-coercively through the processes of cause and effect and human responsibility, God's goal is healing, not hurting. Jesus was clear that sickness is not the result of God's will or punishment for our sins. The message of the Cross and Resurrection is that God feels our pain intimately and confronts the powers of death in our lives and the world with the Energy of Loving Transformation and New Life.

Process theology affirms Jesus' uniqueness as God's healing companion and revelation of Shalom. Process theology also roots Jesus' healing ministry, even the most dramatic healings, in God's universal aim at wholeness and beauty, working within the natural and every process of our cells, organs, emotions, thoughts, and spirits. The heightened naturalism of Jesus' healings invites us to be healers in our own relationships, praying, proclaiming, and touching with the spirit that characterized Jesus' ministry.

Process Healing

Jesus was a medium of God's healing energy. Jesus' touch released the Energy of Love. Even touching Jesus' garments could open persons to God's immanent and ever-present healing power. As John's gospel proclaims, the true light enlightens — and I would add enlivens — everyone (John 1:9).

After a time of silent reflection, prayerfully read Mark 5:25-34, noting its connection to your life:

> Now there was a woman who had been suffering from a flow of blood for twelve years. She had endured much under many physicians and had spent all that she had, and she was no better but rather grew worse. She had heard about Jesus and came up behind him in the crowd and touched his cloak, for she said, "If I but touch his cloak, I will be made well." Immediately her flow of blood stopped, and she felt in her body that she was healed of her disease. Immediately aware that power had gone forth from him, Jesus turned about in the crowd and said, "Who touched my cloak?" And his disciples said to him, "You see the crowd pressing in on you; how can you say, 'Who touched me?'" He looked all around to see who had done it. But the woman, knowing what had happened to her, came in fear and trembling, fell down before him, and told him the whole truth. He said to her, "Daughter, your faith has made you well; go in peace, and be healed of your disease."

What aspects of this scripture speak most directly to your life? How might you creatively awaken God's power coursing through your life and all creation?

At a convenient time, set aside fifteen minutes for contemplative prayer. Begin by breathing deeply God's presence, visualized in terms of a healing light. With each breath, experience God's light filling your body from head to toe, enlivening your whole being. Feel yourself permeated by God's healing light. If there are places of dis-ease, feel God's light bringing healing.

In conclusion, imagine Jesus walking beside you and speaking directly to you — reflecting God's aim at healing — "Beloved one, your faith has made you well; go in peace, and be healed of your disease." Thank God for the divine healing presence in your life and all things.

Chapter Four

Process Theology And Complementary Medicine

The decay of Christianity and Buddhism, as determinative forces in modern thought is due to the fact that each religion has unduly sheltered itself from the other... instead of looking to each other for deeper meanings.[7]

Healing comes in many media from words to touch, acceptance to affirmation. In the course of my life, I have experienced many healings, all undramatic from an observer's perspective, but life-transforming for me, including learning Transcendental Meditation in college led me to embrace a new vision of Christianity; a year later, the affirmation of two pastors in college that inspired me to become a pastor and theologian (vocational healing); responding to hypertension, headaches, and everyday illness through Reiki healing touch and meditation; and caring for a child with cancer through the interplay of chemotherapy and Reiki. In the world envisioned by process theology, whatever touches the spirit transforms the body, and the health of the body shapes our spirit. Today, the adventures of healing cross boundaries between physician and Shaman, chemicals and herbs, and surgery and spiritual practices, as medicine has gone global.

When I was a graduate student, my professor John Cobb wrote a classic on the relationship between Christianity and world religions, titled *Christ in a Pluralistic Age.* Cobb's book remains one of the most important texts in Christology, the study of Christ and Christ's presence in the world, and an inspiration for interfaith dialogue and creative responses to religious and intellectual diversity. In light of the growing edges of health care today, we might supplement Cobb's insights with a complementary title, "Medicine in a Pluralistic Age." The terms "inter-spirituality" and

7 Alfred North Whitehead, *Religion in the Making* (New York: World Publishing, 1972), 140-141.

"hybrid" have entered our vocabularies as descriptive of persons who integrate spiritual practices from a variety of faith traditions. For example, as an active Christian theologian and pastor, I practice Transcendental Meditation, breath prayer, and Reiki Healing touch along with regular preaching, Bible study leadership, practicing Centering Prayer, and leading congregational healing services. I immerse myself in the classics of Christian spirituality and also bathe my spirit in the insights of Thich Nhat Hanh, Rumi, and indigenous Shamans. I learn from Pentecostal healers and Pagan spirit guides. A similar phenomenon occurs in the field of health care. My wife Kate regularly practices Tai Chi, Qigong, Reiki Healing Touch, and is a trained massage therapist. Both of us have received acupuncture and used homeopathic medicines to promote overall well-being.[8] We also take medications, prescribed by our family physician, joining medication with meditation to promote physical and spiritual well-being.

In response to the growing interest in holistic and complementary medicine, the National Office for Complementary and Integrative Health (NCCIH) was created in 1991.[9] The goal of NCCIH is to study various complementary and global medical modalities to determine their benefits. Researchers have often found it challenging to determine the efficacy of various complementary medicines due to 1) lack of double-blind scientific studies and 2) limitations inherent in scientific procedures in terms of detecting the impact of energy work and the power of prayer. Still, scientific studies have identified the following benefits related to complementary medicine: pain relief, both general and in relationship to arthritis; stress reduction; migraine headaches; lowering hypertension; improving balance; shorter hospital stays; and comfort in the context of hospice care. Although not identified specifically as complementary medicine, scientific studies associ-

8 Operating from the principle of "like cures like," homeopathic medicine uses small doses of natural substances that might bring on symptoms in a healthy person to treat a sick person. These small doses trigger the body's natural healing processes.

9 Created in 1991, this affiliate of the National Institutes of Health initially bore the name, Office of Alternative Medicine and then Office of Complementary and Alternative Medicine.

ate recovery from illness, contentment and life satisfaction, overall physical well-being, and lower anxiety when facing death, with regular church attendance and volunteering.

Process theology affirms that God's aim at beauty, well-being, and intensity of experience is universal. Wherever healing is present, and whatever practices promote healing, God is its source. Just as God is present as the ultimate inspiration for the varieties of religious experience and the world's religious traditions, God is also at work in the many modalities of healing, technological, surgical, chemical, energetic, hands-on, psychological, liturgical laying on of hands, yogic, nutritional, herbal, and shamanic. While the value of each modality must be assessed as thoroughly as possible, recipients of these treatments attest to their value and regularly combine them with Western technological medical care. Given the universality of divine inspiration and healing, the various modalities must not be "sheltered" from each other, but, as Whitehead counsels, look "to each other for deeper meanings," especially in relationship to chronic, debilitating, and life-threatening diseases and the relief of chronic pain. We must go beyond dualism to join high tech and high touch and to integrate science and spirituality to promote healing and wholeness.

The Heart of Complementary Medicine. The first physicians, indigenous healers, treated the whole person and their relationships. Like Jesus, they believed that spirituality, and that the impact of "spirits," could be a matter of life and death. They used poultices and plants, herbs and dream interpretation, and also incantations and exorcisms. They focused on the bodily symptoms and also issues of meaning, relationship, ethics, and faith. Like all medicinal procedures, even Western medicine, they utilized the power of faith — the placebo effect — to heal their patients along with "folk remedies." This same holistic spirit is emerging in whole person medicine today, whether in responding to migraines or cancer. Technology and touch, and chemical therapy and contemplation, complement each other in promoting health and addressing sickness.

Although there are many shared characteristics among the various forms of complementary medicine, the following appear most universal in describing the heart of complementary medicine:

» *Spirituality* — the recognition of the spiritual component of health and illness, and the need to treat illnesses spiritually as well as physically.
» *Energy* — the importance of releasing, unblocking, and balancing the energy (chi, ki, dunamis) that flows in and through us.
» *Touch* — the importance of touch to comfort and mediate divine healing energy.
» *Natural, non-invasive* — utilizing the body's innate healing capacity to maintain health and treat illness.
» *Emphasis on agency* — empowering persons to be active in their own healing in partnership with other healers.
» *Response to birth and death* — birth and death are spiritual and relational as well as physical events and need to be treated using spiritual as well as medical arts.

The medicine of the future sees healing as global and holistic, personal and planetary, and elicits the inherent healing powers, the Energy of Love, flowing in and through each of us.

Process Healing

Jesus once joined prayer and saliva, a first-century medicinal, to cure a sight-impaired man, demonstrating that spirituality and medicine complement each other in the healing process. The future of medical healing involves the relationship of technology, touch, energy, and spirituality, not in opposition but in employing the gifts of each of these divinely inspired modalities. The divine aim at beauty and wholeness embraces a wide range of healing practices. However, it is important to note that these are best used to complement each other. One should not discontinue a pharmaceutical treatment or reject a surgery without consultation with a wise health care professional.

Taking your medicine in a healing way. Most persons take some form of health supplement or medication, whether pharmaceutical or natural. In this exercise, take your medicine in a healing way by joining prayer with your pills or remedies. As you take your "medication," open to God's healing presence, and give thanks for the healing power of herbs, vitamins, and pharmaceuticals, and ask that the "medication" promote your wellbeing so that you can be a more effective companion in God's quest to heal the world.

High touch. If you have not received a hands-on healing treatment, you may wish to make an appointment with a hands-on healer to receive a therapeutic touch, healing touch, or Reiki Healing Touch treatment. Experience the power of healing touch to connect you with the Energy of Love.

Whether or not you are trained in a healing touch modality, you may use touch to promote your own well-being. Find a comfortable and quiet place to lie down. Take a few minutes to be still as you invoke God's healing presence. Breathe slowly and deeply feeling God's healing entering you with each breath. Visualize God's Energy of Love flowing into your hands. Notice any changes in your perception of your hands. Are they tingling or warmer? Don't worry if you don't feel anything special. Apply your hands to the top of your head and simply hold them there for a minute, feeling the touch of your skin and breathing healing into your body. Now place your hands in succession, for a minute or so, on your face and eyes, throat, heart, stomach, above your genitals. Enjoy the feel of touch and your desire to be a companion in affirming your body and promoting your overall wellbeing. Conclude with a prayer of thanksgiving for God's healing energy and for God's continuing presence as your healing companion.

Chapter Five

Healing The Dying

At the heart of the nature of things, there are always the dream of youth and the harvest of tragedy. The Adventure of the Universe starts with the dream and reaps Tragic Beauty. This is the secret of the union of Zest with Peace: - That the suffering attains its end in a Harmony of Harmonies. The immediate experience of this Final Fact, with its union of Youth and Tragedy, is the sense of Peace. In this way the world receives its persuasion toward such perfections as are possible for its diverse individual occasions.[10]

Protestant Reformer Martin Luther once declared, "In the midst of life, we are surrounded by death." Process-relational theology more boldly states that life is a constant movement of perpetual perishing. You can't step in the same river twice. As Whitehead says, "no thinker thinks twice; and, to put the matter more generally, no subject experiences twice."[11] Each moment of experience dies in the process of giving birth to its successors. The reality of perpetual perishing can be seen as life's greatest evil, as Whitehead avers. It can also be the source of creative transformation, spiritual adventure, and personal and relational healing. Death is inevitable. The mortality rate remains at 100%, despite our technological interventions and commitment to healing practices. Our need for healing, for a sense of wholeness and peace, is necessitated by the fact that death is inevitable for us and everyone we love, including the planet and solar system upon which our lives depend.

Process spirituality embraces the reality of death as the pathway to enlightenment, transformation, and resurrection. We are star stuff, children of the Big Bang and the Cosmic Adventure, and to the stars and earth we will eventually return. Spiritual practices

10 Alfred North Whitehead, *Adventures of Ideas* (New York: Free Press, 1969), 296.

11 Alfred North Whitehead, *Process and Reality*, 29.

enable us to embrace our mortality, trusting with Martin Luther, that "in the midst of death, we are surrounded by life." Process theology proclaims that when there cannot be a cure, there can always be a healing, and within every death lies the promise of resurrection. The healing process at life's descending edges involves acceptance of the reality of death, and trust that our perpetually perishing lives live on in God's Holy Adventure. Dust to dust and ashes to ashes were never spoken of the Spirit that moves through our lives and all creation.

Every great spiritual teacher wrestles with the reality of death. Moses looks toward the horizon of the Promised Land. Knowing that although he will never set foot there, he trusts that God will continue to inspire and challenge the people he led. The Hindu sages discovered immortality in the human spirit, and the inner spirit of all things, connecting perpetual perishing physical world with eternal being, consciousness, and bliss. Gautama the Buddha taught a path of liberation, taking us beyond suffering born of attachment to permanence and stability in an ever-changing world. Agnostic about the afterlife, Gautama nevertheless taught a way of acceptance and calm that enables us to live joyfully in the face of life's constant changes. Jesus faces the Cross, was tempted to avoid the pain and indignity of execution but trusted his spirit to God's Spirit. In Jesus' resurrection, his followers discover hope and new life that transcends any threat, including martyrdom, they will face in this lifetime.

Process theology finds healing in facing death through the interplay of acceptance and hope. Denial of death and hopelessness in facing death, both personal and planetary, paralyze the spirit, diminish the vitality of life, and tempt us to seek immortality in ways that harm ourselves and the planet. In contrast, process theology counsels us to embrace the perpetual perishing nature of life, treasuring each moment, embracing grief and joy, enlarging our spirits, and trusting the future to God's Loving Embrace.

In my own embodiment of process-relational spirituality, I begin each day with two contrasting affirmations: "This is the day that God has made, and I will rejoice and be glad in it" and "Now is only the moment there is. I will live today as if this is my last day on earth." These affirmations join gratitude and delight in awakening to a new day and its possibilities, with claiming the significance of each passing moment, knowing that all things will pass, and that I want to be fully alive in this mortal moment in time. The final chapter of this text cites Bernard Loomer's definition of stature, or spiritual size, as "the volume of life you can take into your being and still maintain your integrity and individuality, the intensity and variety of outlook you can entertain in the unity of your being without feeling defensive or insecure." Healing comes from embracing the fullness of life, including death, as part of God's Holy Adventure. We are healed by abundant living in the present and hope for everlasting life in companionship with God. Creatures of dust and star stuff we return to the Creative Process. Creatures of Spirit, we live on in terms of God's Memory and our companionship with the One Who Loved Us and the Universe into Life. Healing in the face of death comes from embracing life in all its tragic beauty.

While healing the dying does not require belief in survival after death, process theology affirms two kinds of immortality — objective and subjective. Objective immortality is our life in God's evolving memory and involvement in the world. God is the one to whom all hearts are open and all desires are known. God treasures each moment of experience in God's ever-expanding embrace of creation, described by Whitehead as God's consequent nature. Our lives perish, moment by moment, and live evermore in God's memory, becoming the materials for God's loving creativity in the ongoing history of the universe. Our trust is in the Everlasting One and not our longevity. Our lives are our gifts to God, and "doing something beautiful for God" is enough to give life meaning. In transcending self-interest and isolated individuality and embracing world loyalty, we see our small as part of God's Great Self. We experience a type of *theosis,* or divinization, in which we embody the spirit of the Bodhisattva, who forgoes enlightenment, until all are released from suffering, and the Christ, who dies to self so that the True Self be resurrected.

The marriage of objective and subjective immortality that I envision as a process theologian avoids the dualism of this life and the afterlife. What we do today matters to God and to the world beyond us. Our afterlife and the afterlives of others are shaped by our actions today, that is, our actions shape our and others' identities which continue beyond the grave. The love of this world passes into God's nature and into any afterlife we can imagine, bridging the ethical gulf between this life and the next.

One of my favorite hymns proclaims, "my life goes on in endless song above life's lamentations, I hear the sweet, though far-off hymn that hails a new creation…No storm can shake my inmost calm while to that refuge clinging since Christ is Lord of heaven and earth, how can I keep from singing?"[12] Although process theologians have been modest in reflecting on survival after death, I believe that process theology provides a creative vision of the afterlife as a continuing holy adventure. While we see in a mirror dimly, as the Apostle Paul confesses, I believe that healing in everlasting life involves the following affirmations:

- God's love is everlasting and embraces all creation.
- God's love overcomes imperfection and sin and provides a path toward wholeness beyond this lifetime that joins justice with spiritual transformation.
- We live on eternally and find wholeness in God's everlasting love.
- We contribute to our own and others' everlasting journey by what we do today.
- The afterlife is a time of continuing growth, adventure, and self-transcendence in which we will experience and embody new possibilities on the path to becoming the glory of God, fully alive beings.
- The afterlife will involve an environment in which we are transparent to God's vision and will evolve toward our fullest life without environmental obstruction.

Near-death experiences alert us to the possibility that death is the beginning of a new phase in our spiritual journeys. Christ's resurrection testifies to the holistic nature of the afterlife as relational and expansive. In the afterlife, we become "more" rather than less of what we are in this lifetime, with new forms of re-

12 Robert Lowry, "How Can I Keep From Singing."

lationship, communication, and embodiment. Process theology is agnostic questions such as, "Do only humans have everlasting life? Will our companion animals as well as Right Whales and chimpanzees experience post-mortem adventures? Will simpler life forms also share in everlasting life?" Certainly, everything that exists will live in on God's consequent nature as objectively immortal, but will that immortality have a subjective, experiential shape? Moreover, process theology does not weigh in as to which vision of survival after death is more realistic: the Western vision of one life and then heavenly beatitude or the image of the afterlife in terms of reincarnation, of many lifetimes in evolving toward experiencing our inherent divinity. My vision of the afterlife as an evolving journey involving growth, adventure, and new tasks to accomplish, joins the insights of the heavenly realm and the journey of reincarnation.

Healing the dying involves trust that the impact of our lives goes beyond this moment or this lifetime. Meaning comes from mattering to God and the ongoing universe. In the spirit of Jesus, those who cling to their small selves, and to self-interested individualism, will lose their lives, will be terrified at the prospect of death, while those who lose their lives, who die to self to be reborn in transpersonal openness to the Self of the Universe will know that whether they live or die they belong to God.

There is judgment in life but the accounting is loving and healing. When we see the impact of our lives, we will be given the grace and energy to choose transformation and wholeness and empathy with all creation. We may defer our divinization or enlightenment by our agency, even in the afterlife, but as a friend's sweatshirt proclaims, "God loves me, and there's nothing I can do about it!" Truly love never ends, and love is, as Thornton Wilder asserts, the bridge between this life and eternity. Nothing can separate us from the love of God! How can we keep from singing!

Process Healing

Process theology affirms the imagery of Bonaventure and Nicholas of Cusa: God is an infinite circle or sphere "whose center is everywhere and whose circumference is nowhere." God centers each one of us with the energy of loving possibility. Divine energy and love are our deepest realities. God's loving embrace encircles everything that has been, is now, and will be forever. Love never ends.

In this exercise, visualize God's loving flowing in and through you, filling you with love and light. See yourself as transparent to divinity emerging from the birth of the universe and continuing onto infinity. Imagine yourself connected by this energy of love to all creation, one in spirit and flesh, yet unique in all the universe. Feel the energy embracing you, enveloping you, expanding you, until you feel yourself filled with divine love, a unique self, connected with the Self of All Things. Ponder your life uniting with the Heartbeat of the Universe and growing in grace with God as your companion. Examining your life, ponder what is currently incomplete in your life? What needs healing? What needs to expand and grow? What needs to be forgiven and made new? Let God's loving energy wash over all your limitations and imperfections filling you with wholeness?

Reflect a moment on those whom you would like to meet in "heaven." Experience yourself sharing affection and intimacy, learning together, growing and forgiving, as companions in God's Never-ending Holy Adventure.

Chapter Six

Healing The Person, Healing The Planet

By size I mean the stature of a person's soul, the range and depth of his love, his capacity for relationships. I mean the volume of life you can take into your being and still maintain your integrity and individuality, the intensity and variety of outlook you can entertain in the unity of your being without feeling defensive or insecure. I mean the strength of your spirit to encourage others to become freer in the development of their diversity and uniqueness.[13]

Talmudic wisdom proclaims that "if you save one life, it is as if you are saving the whole world." Conversely, "if you destroy one life, it is as if you are destroying the whole world." Process theology proclaims the intricate interdependence of all life. There is no "other," separate and alien from myself. We are bound together, and what brings authentic fulfillment to me enriches the world. I am enriched by the well-being of others, whether in Sudan, Ukraine, Taiwan, or Guatemala. My well-being is connected to that of a young man killed by the police in Memphis, a transgender person maligned by a politician, an aimless youth caught up in racist conspiracy theories, or children forbidden to learn their racial history by demagogues. Acts of evil anywhere diminish my life as well as those who are harmed and those who perpetrate them. Times are challenging and process theologians want us to recognize that we are not only in the same storm, but that we should see ourselves in the same boat. Process-relational thought is foreshadowed by the Apostle Paul's vision of the body of Christ, in which every part needs the others, diversity is a gift, and the flourishing of one and all is interconnection. As this first century proto-process theologian avers, "if one member suffers, all suffer

13 Bernard Loomer, "S-I-Z-E is the Measure," Henry James Cargas and Bernard Lee, *Religious Experiences and Process Theology* (Mahweh, NJ: Paulist Press, 1976), 70.

together with it; if one member is honored, all rejoice together with it." (I Corinthians 1:27)

Process theology proclaims that all health is community health, and all medicine is community medicine. More than that, in our fragile planet, all health is planetary. Climate change puts humankind at risk through drought, hurricane, severe weather, and the fight for water and food. Millions are climate refugees, many of which suffer from life-threatening malnutrition and dehydration. Children who survive malnutrition, whether the result of climate change, political upheaval, or economic injustice, live with diminished possibilities, including human-caused intellectual handicaps. In the United States, gun violence is a public health emergency, tearing apart homes and schools, as well as city streets and rural thoroughfares.

In reflecting on the dynamic interdependence of life, Whitehead states, "if we are fussily exact, we cannot define where a body begins and where external nature ends…the human body is that region of the world which is the primary field of human expressions." Think about your own health and healing process and the many ways it is dependent on your environment: air and water quality, economic and political stability, supply chains, workplace, educational opportunities, and support and acceptance by others. The whole universe conspires to create each moment of experience, and the greatest positive or negative impact comes from our immediate environment.

You cannot separate mysticism, healing, and prophetic challenge. From a process perspective, our experiences of God as the heartbeat of our lives and the vital force residing in all things awakens our self-awareness and our need for healing. It also deepens our empathy so that we are attuned to the joys and sorrows of others. Spiritual experiences align us with the Heartbeat of the Universe, the "fellow sufferer who understands" and the intimate companion who celebrates. Aware of the currents of the Great Empath moving through our lives, inspiring the spiritual and moral arcs of history, we are sensitized to the pain of others and inspired to challenge the unnecessary destruction of any creature.

Experience and value are universal, and so is ethical consideration. As Whitehead observes:

> Everything has some value for itself, for others, and for the whole. This characterizes the meaning of actuality. By reason of this character, constituting reality, the concept of morals arises. We have no right to deface the value experiences which is the very essence of the universe. Existence, in its very nature, is the upholding of value intensity.[14]

Following the spirit of his Hebraic parents, Jesus counseled "love your neighbor as yourself." Healing starts with my wellbeing, body, mind, spirit, and relationships. As Rabbi Hillel proclaims, "If I am not for myself, who will be for me?" In authentically loving yourself, you aim at incarnating the glory of God, a fully alive human, through spiritual practices, self-care, positive relationships, realizing of personal gifts, and opening to God's healing energy of love. You seek to be a healed, not just wounded, healer. Your healing contributes to the healing of the world. Rabbi Hillel continues, "If I am only for myself, what am I?" Abundant life is a shared experience. In the intricate garment of human and planetary destiny, "I cannot be what I ought to be until you are what you ought to be. And you can never be what you ought to be until I am what I ought to be. That's the way the God's universe is made."[15] In loving others and providing for the basics necessary for their physical, spiritual, economic, and emotional well-being, I live out my full humanity. In letting go of our isolated individualistic selves, and their closed system world, we open to the energies of God's open system universe.

Rabbi Hillel concludes his counsel with, "If not now, when?" This is the day that God has made! Now is the moment of salvation! Process theology challenges us to go beyond self-interest to embrace world loyalty. Shalom, the dream of peace and wholeness, providing a platform for to healthy persons and communities, will not come from individualistic self-absorption or national self-regard. As unrealistic as it may seem, persons and nations

---

14 *Modes of Thought* (New York: Free Press, 1968), 111.

15 Martin Luther King, *A Knock at Midnight* (New York: Warner Books, 2000), 208.

are challenged to become God's companions in healing the earth, establishing an infrastructure of well-being that is planetary and transnational. In healing ourselves and relationships, we heal the world, and in healing the world, we heal ourselves.

Process Healing

Planetary and personal healing are interdependent. When we heal ourselves through our openness to God's energy of love, we create a healing field of force that tips the balance of relational and planetary life toward wholeness. Conversely, the creation of healing environments, respectful of persons, committed to justice and wellbeing, and planetary health, contributes to personal flourishing in body, mind, spirit, and relationships. Anxiety about the future, along with injustice, poverty, racism, and marginalization, promotes depression, hopelessness, and passivity, that diminishes our cellular and spiritual vitality. Moreover, those who commit injustice, as Jesus says, are in danger of losing their souls. Racism hurts the souls of those who perpetrate racial injustice.

This exercise builds on the healing process described in Chapter Five. Once again, find yourself a quiet and comfortable place. Begin to breathe slowly and deeply, visualizing healing light entering your body, and illumining it from head to toe, enlivening and enlightening your spiritual, intellectual, and emotional life. Let this light of God fill you to the extent that you begin to "shine" (Matthew 5:14-16). Now, as you exhale with each breath, send your light out into the world. Experience the light of God flowing through you illuminating the world: your family, neighborhood, region, nation, and the planet. Remember that you are connected with all things and that as their light brightens, so does yours.

In your imagination, feel your healing light joined with a situation or place that needs healing: Right Whale pups, inner city and Appalachian children, icebergs, refugee camps, children on the USA borderlands, and so forth. In a time of reflection, open to God's guidance, as you seek guidance to join your gifts with the world's needs. If something comes to you in this exercise, make a commitment to research the situation that inspires you as a prelude to service. Become a healed healer, for God's and your neighbor's sake.

Let us conclude this text with prayer.
Healing God, align my spirit with your quest for global healing. Awaken me to your healing touch and to share in your healing through compassionate service, touch, and intercessory prayer. Open me to your grace so that I might embrace my calling as your companion in healing the earth.
Amen.

Reading for Healing

Rita Nakashima Brock, *Journeys By Heart: A Christology of Erotic Power,* (Wipf and Stock, 2008).

Larry Dossey, *Healing Words,* (HarperOne, 1995).

Bruce Epperly, *101 Soul Seeds for Healing and Wholeness,* (Anamchara, 2021).

Bruce Epperly, *A Center in the Cyclone: 21st Century Clergy Selfcare,* (Rowman and Littlefield, 2014).

Bruce Epperly, *The Energy of Love: Reiki and Christian Healing,* (Energion, 2017).

Bruce Epperly, *God's Touch: Faith, Wholeness, and the Healing Miracles of Jesus,* (Westminster/John Knox, 2001).

Bruce Epperly, *Healing Marks: Healing and Spirituality in Mark's Gospel,* (Energion, 2012).

Bruce Epperly, *Process Spirituality: Practicing Holy Adventure,* (Energion, 2017).

Bruce Epperly, *Reiki Healing Touch and the Way of Jesus,* (Northstone Books, 2005).

Bruce Epperly, *Healing Worship: Purpose and Practice,* (Pilgrim Press, 2006).

Thich Nhat Hanh, *The Energy of Prayer*, (Parallax, 2006).

Morton Kelsey, *Psychology, Medicine, and Christian Healing,* (Harper Collins, 1988).

Dale Matthews, *The Faith Factor: God, Medicine, and Healing,* (Viking, 1988).

Tilda Norberg and Robert Webber, *Stretch Out Your Hand: Exploring Healing Prayer,* (Upper Room Books, 1998).

www.ingramcontent.com/pod-product-compliance
Lightning Source LLC
LaVergne TN
LVHW030913080826
845145LV00010B/2875
* 9 7 8 1 6 3 1 9 9 8 8 9 8 *